EASY WRAPS & ROLLS

EASY WRAPS & ROLLS
20 simple and stylish ideas shown in 150 photographs

JENNI FLEETWOOD

LORENZ BOOKS

This edition is published by Lorenz Books, an imprint of Anness Publishing Ltd, Blaby Road, Wigston, Leicestershire LE18 4SE; info@anness.com

www.lorenzbooks.com; www.annesspublishing.com

If you like the images in this book and would like to investigate using them for publishing, promotions or advertising, please visit our website www.practicalpictures.com for more information.

© Anness Publishing Ltd 2013

All rights reserved. No part of this publication may be reproduced, stored in a retrieval system, or transmitted in any way or by any means, electronic, mechanical, photocopying, recording or otherwise, without the prior written permission of the copyright holder.

PUBLISHER: Joanna Lorenz
MANAGING EDITOR: Linda Fraser
SENIOR EDITOR: Margaret Malone
DESIGN: SteersMcGillan Ltd
PHOTOGRAPHER: William Lingwood
HOME ECONOMIST: Becky Johnson
STYLIST: Helen Trent
ADDITIONAL RECIPES: Catherine Atkinson, Jacqueline Clarke, Joanna Farrow, Yasuko Fukuoka, Nicola Graimes, Kathy Man, Jane Milton, Sallie Morris and Kate Whiteman
ADDITIONAL PHOTOGRAPHY: Nicki Dowey, Gus Filgate, Michelle Garrett, Thomas Odulate, Craig Robertson and Simon Smith
JACKET PHOTOGRAPHY: Martin Brigdale
PRODUCTION CONTROLLER: Mai-Ling Collyer

NOTES
• Bracketed terms are intended for American readers.
• For all recipes, quantities are given in both metric and imperial measures and, where appropriate, in standard cups and spoons. Follow one set of measures, but not a mixture, because they are not interchangeable.
• Standard spoon and cup measures are level. 1 tsp = 5ml, 1 tbsp = 15ml, 1 cup = 250ml/8fl oz.
• Australian standard tablespoons are 20ml. Australian readers should use 3 tsp in place of 1 tbsp for measuring small quantities.
• American pints are 16fl oz/2 cups. American readers should use 20fl oz/ 2.5 cups in place of 1 pint when measuring liquids.
• Electric oven temperatures in this book are for conventional ovens. When using a fan oven, the temperature will probably need to be reduced by about 10–20°C/20–40°F. Since ovens vary, you should check with your manufacturer's instruction book for guidance.
• Medium (US large) eggs are used unless otherwise stated.

Front cover shows Lamb Kebab Wraps with Moroccan Spiced Courgettes – for recipe, see page 49

PUBLISHER'S NOTE
Although the advice and information in this book are believed to be accurate and true at the time of going to press, neither the authors nor the publisher can accept any legal responsibility or liability for any errors or omissions that may have been made nor for any inaccuracies nor for any loss, harm or injury that comes about from following instructions or advice in this book.

Contents

Introduction	6
Essential wraps	8
Preparation and wrapping techniques	10
Fabulous ways with fillings and sauces	12
Snacks and appetizers	14
Lunchtime wraps	30
Gourmet wraps	46
Index	64

Introduction

Good things come in small packages and, when it comes to wraps, the old adage is entirely accurate. Wraps are pretty, practical and ideal for all occasions, from breakfast on the run to a stylish supper with friends. There's an element of excitement in opening a beautifully presented parcel, especially when the contents are very good to eat.

Most people associate tortillas with savoury Mexican food, but they are far more versatile than that. They are ideal vehicles for salads, stir-fries – even sushi – and they are perfect for a working lunch. While the tortilla warms, you can raid the refrigerator for fillings, then bring all your creativity to bear in making a great snack. They also make delicious desserts when filled with fruit and topped with a rich chocolate sauce.

Although tortillas are the obvious choice when it comes to wrapping, there are plenty of exciting alternatives. Crêpes and pancakes (from East and West), lettuce and cabbage leaves, wafer-thin sheets of nori seaweed and even inedible corn husks can all be used to impressive effect.

Enclosing food in its own parcel is a great activity for all the family, and a wonderful way of introducing children to the pleasure of putting together a tasty meal. While they compete to see who can fold the neatest burrito, or create the most colourful fajita, you can ensure that the ingredients on offer meet their nutritional needs.

Wrapping is easy, it's fun and everyone can do it. For inspiration, just turn the page. This book contains all you need to know about the different types of wraps available, plus step-by-step instructions for filling and folding, and great tips for quick and easy fillings. It'll give you a whole new perspective on packaged food.

Essential wraps

Wraps come in all sorts of guises, from lettuce and lotus leaves to the more familiar tortillas and pancakes.

Tortillas

Probably the most popular wrap of all is the tortilla. There are two basic types – wheat flour and corn. Wheat flour tortillas are widely sold in supermarkets, usually in vacuum-sealed packs of six or eight. Large tortillas measure 20–25cm/ 8–10in. For snacks and first courses, the smaller 14cm/5½in tortillas are ideal.

Also look out for tortilla wraps. These are thinner than traditional tortillas, making them easier to roll and more suitable for light fillings. They come in several flavours, including spicy tomato and nacho cheese. Corn tortillas may be sold fresh in the bakery section of food stores, and are available in vacuum-sealed packs from supermarkets.

Asian pancakes

These are made from plain dough rather than a batter and include a number of different types. The thinner rounds – also known as mandarin pancakes – are traditionally served with Peking duck. Spring roll wrappers are square and come in three sizes: small, medium and large. The most useful size for wraps is medium. These measure 23cm/9in square and come in packs of 20 sheets. Spring roll wrappers are cooked after being filled, by deep-frying or steaming.

Another type is the rice paper pancake, which is made from a rice flour dough and can be served uncooked. The dough is rolled out until it is paper thin, cut into rounds, then sun-dried. The pancakes are dry and need to be handled with care. Before use, they should be softened with water, which turns them translucent.

Small Asian wonton skins are useful as cocktail wraps. They are made from a flour and egg dough. Most are

square, although you can buy round ones. If you use frozen ones, ensure that they are thawed before use, or they will stick together. Like spring rolls, wonton skins are cooked after being filled.

Chapatis

Made from wholemeal (whole-wheat) flour called *ata*, Indian chapatis are traditionally brushed with ghee before being cooked on a *java* or cast iron griddle. Available in packs of six, they measure about 20cm/8in across. Not surprisingly, these flavoursome wrappers are best prepared with a spicy filling, such as rogan josh or strips of tandoori chicken, and served with a generous dollop of plain yogurt on top.

Pancakes and crêpes

Making pancakes takes very little time, but for spur-of-the-moment sweet and savoury wraps, keep a pack of pancakes in the refrigerator or freezer. Traditional 15cm/6in pancakes are available in packets of six. Some stores also sell traditional sweet crêpes from Brittany. These are about 30cm/12in across and come folded in four. Omelettes can also be used as wraps, but these need to be made fresh.

Vegetables and leaves

There are quite a number of vegetables and leaves that make handy wrappers. Aubergines (eggplant) and courgettes (zucchini) are two excellent choices. Slice them lengthways, cook in olive oil, then drain and wrap around your chosen filling. Tomatoes, olives, feta cheese and herbs such as oregano and basil go well with these Mediterranean vegetables.

Lettuce leaves can be used fresh, as scoops for tabbouleh mixtures or dips, or the leaves can be blanched and used as wraps. They have a subtle flavour and delicate texture, making the leaves particularly appropriate for fish dishes. Spinach leaves can also be used in this way. Cabbage leaves are more robust, and taste great when rolled around a meat filling and braised in stock.

Vine leaves are edible. In Greece and the Lebanon, where they are widely used, they are filled with rice and occasionally meat or fish.  Vine leaves preserved in brine are available in packets and cans. They must be rinsed thoroughly in cold water, then blanched before use. Fresh leaves only need a swift rinse before being blanched. To freeze, pack the raw leaves in a container and cover. When needed, plunge the frozen leaves into boiling water for 1–2 minutes, then drain.

 Lotus leaves are not very well known outside of Thailand, where they are used for wrapping savoury and sweet fillings for steaming and also for flavouring. The huge leaves – up to 38cm/15in across – are sometimes available fresh but are usually sold dried from Asian stores.

Corn husks, like lotus leaves, are used purely for wrapping, and are not eaten. They make wonderfully rustic-looking parcels, which look even more interesting if tied with a strip of corn husk.

Nori is wafer-thin, dried seaweed. It is mainly sold as a wrapper for sushi, and is available from Asian stores. For rolling sushi, nori must be supported on a bamboo mat or in the hand, though enclosing it in a tortilla, and then rolling it up, makes this unnecessary.

Bread wraps

Unleavened breads from the Middle East are ideal for wrapping. Examples include lavash and mankoush. Sliced white bread makes a good wrap if you cut the crusts off, then flatten each slice by placing it between sheets of clear film (plastic wrap) and pressing with a rolling pin. The same technique can be used for the sweet Italian yeast bread, panettone.

Essential wraps

Preparation and wrapping techniques

Below are some of the most common ways to prepare and fold wraps, but don't let that stop you from inventing your own.

Tortillas
It is important to warm tortillas before folding them, or they will tear or crack. To microwave, remove them from their packaging, separate and cover with clear film (plastic wrap). Microwave on Full Power. One tortilla will take 8 seconds; six will take 45–60 seconds.

Filling and folding tortillas

Burritos are the classic tortilla wrap. To make, put the filling on the lower half of the tortilla, keeping it within an area measuring 13 x 5cm/5 x 2in. Fold the sides of the tortilla towards the centre, then bring the bottom edge up. Roll the tortilla up until the filling is fully enclosed, then fold the top down, envelope fashion.

Fajitas are made by bringing up the bottom and folding in the sides of a filled tortilla, so that the tortilla is open at one end.
Hot fillings are usual, such as strips of sizzling chicken or beef with onions.

 Chimichangas are a third type of tortilla envelope. They are made by piling the filling in the centre, then folding in the bottom, sides and top, so that a square package results. This is then held in place with a wooden cocktail stick (toothpick), and fried in hot oil until crisp.

Enchiladas are rolls made from corn or wheat tortillas. The filling is placed in the centre of the tortilla, rolled up and placed in a baking dish. More rolls are added, in a single layer, and sauce is poured over the top before baking.

Flautas are thin rolls, made from corn tortillas. They are deep-fried after filling.

Quesadillas are half moon shaped tortilla wraps. To make, place a tortilla in a frying pan to warm, then spread it with some spicy salsa. Place a filling of meat and cheese on one half of the tortilla, fold the top over, and cook for 2 minutes.

Although there are several variations, there are basically only three ways of folding a filled tortilla: the envelope, the roll and the half moon. In Mexico, these go by various names, depending on the filling, the folding method and whether the filled tortilla is later deep-fried. The following are the traditional shapes:

Asian pancakes

Steaming or simply soaking in water makes these pancakes easy to use.

Reheating mandarin pancakes

Serve these thin pancakes piping hot with the fillings of your choice.
1 Stack the pancakes, interleaving them with squares of baking parchment.
2 Carefully wrap the stacked pancakes in foil, folding over the sides of the foil so that the pancakes are completely sealed.
3 Put the parcel in a steamer and cover. Place on a trivet in a wok of simmering water. Steam for about 5 minutes, or until hot.

Preparing rice paper pancakes

When softened in water, rice paper pancakes can be folded around a filling.
1 Fill a bowl with warm water. Dip each pancake in the water for a few seconds, or until translucent, then place on a board. Arrange the filling in the centre.
2 Fold the sides across the filling and fold the bottom part up to cover it, then arrange attractive ingredients such as shrimps or fresh herbs on top. Bring the final flap over, and dampen the edges to seal. Serve at once with a dipping sauce.

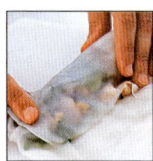

Chapatis, pancakes and crêpes

These simple breads and pancakes are best served warm. Thaw frozen ones for 2 hours at room temperature before using. To heat pancakes or crêpes, wrap them in foil, support on a baking sheet and place in an oven preheated to 200°C/400°F/Gas 6 for 10 minutes. To heat chapatis, sprinkle them lightly with water and bake at 180°C/350°F/Gas 4 for 2–3 minutes, or grill (broil) for 30 seconds on each side.

Folding pancakes and crêpes

Large pancakes and crêpes can be folded in the same way as tortillas, but smaller ones are best rolled around the filling and secured in place with a cocktail stick. If the filling is light, such as a flavoured butter, the pancakes or crêpes can be folded in four. Chapatis are too thick for any elaborate wrapping. Simply fold them over the filling and serve at once.

Storing and freezing wraps

Tortillas, pancakes and crêpes in vacuum packs can be kept for a few days in a cool, dry place, or frozen.

Spring roll wrappers, wonton skins and mandarin pancakes can all be frozen. Rice paper pancakes do not need to be frozen. As long as the packages are tightly sealed, they will keep for months in a cool, dry place.

Home-made pancakes of all types can be interleaved with sheets of baking parchment, wrapped in a foil parcel and frozen. Bought pancakes and crêpes can also be frozen.

All frozen wraps must be thawed thoroughly before use.

Vegetables and leaves

Most of the vegetables and leaves used for wrapping are easy to prepare but corn husks may be unfamiliar.

Preparing and using corn husks

1 Soak the dried corn husks in a bowl of cold water for 10 minutes, then drain the husks and wipe the white residue from the leaves. Soak in boiling water until soft; pat dry with kitchen paper.
2 Place the husks flat on a dry surface. Place the filling in the centre, wrap, then tie in neat parcels before steaming.

Fabulous ways with fillings and sauces

Tex-Mex ingredients are classic fillings for wraps. Although these are delicious, there are many more superb options.

There are no rules when choosing a filling, but some combinations will make for more successful wrapping.

Balancing moisture and texture
In the same way that you would butter bread for a sandwich, add moisture to a wrap by spreading the tortilla with a salsa, mayonnaise or softened cream cheese, or top the filling with sour cream. If it is a

sweet wrap, pour over a sauce, or serve with thick yogurt or crème fraîche. When filling the wrap, try not to overfill. Use about 300ml/½ pint/1¼ cups for a large savoury tortilla; half that amount if the filling is sweet.

Ingredients need to complement each other, not just in terms of taste, but also as regards texture. Balance tuna with cucumber; a meat mixture with crisp lettuce; lightly poached pears with nuts such as almonds. Experiment with lots of different types of wraps – try salad leaves, spinach, nori and vine leaves.

Ideas for quick and easy wraps
Breakfast on a pancake or plain tortilla wrapped around a filling made by mixing muesli with Greek (US strained plain) yogurt, chopped fresh dates, chopped apple and perhaps a little honey. Serve extra yogurt and honey on the side.

Try a tortilla wrap with a filling of blue cheese such as Roquefort mashed with soft white (farmer's) cheese and sliced pears or fresh fennel. For green stuff, add some lamb's lettuce or romaine. Top with chopped walnuts, or add crunch with sliced celery or green (bell) pepper.

For a fast lunch, tuna makes a great filling. Spread a warmed tortilla with a little mayonnaise. Top with drained canned tuna, some shredded lettuce and a few slices of fresh peach. Roll and serve.

A really healthy option is to mix plain or flavoured couscous with some diced cucumber, finely chopped tomato, spring onions (scallions) and plenty of chopped fresh mint. When filling the warmed tortilla, add a few cubes of feta cheese.

Drain a can of asparagus spears and set the best eight spears aside. Chop the rest and mix with soft white (farmer's) cheese. Stir in a little grated Parmesan and season. Spread on warmed small tortillas and top with some asparagus spears and extra cheese. Roll and serve.

For a meat option, roll the asparagus spears in the previous combination in prosciutto before adding to the wrap.

Stir-fry strips of chicken breast fillets with slices of red and yellow (bell) pepper. Fill warmed tortillas with the mixture, with a spoonful of sour cream.

Cut the crusts from 12 square slices of brown bread. Round one corner of each slice. Spread four slices with soft white (farmer's) cheese mixed with chives, four slices with guacamole and four slices with mackerel or smoked salmon pâté. Roll up into a cone, with the rounded area at the base. Secure with a cocktail stick (toothpick) and chill for 20 minutes. When ready to serve, remove the cocktail sticks and garnish with a few sprigs of fresh salad herbs.

Dipping sauces and salsas

Sauces make perfect partners for wraps. Here are four simple suggestions that are ideal with any number of wraps.

Ginger and soy sauce

This sauce tastes great with filled rice paper pancakes, especially those that feature prawns (shrimp).

1 Mix 60ml/4 tbsp red wine vinegar with about 7.5ml/ 1½ tsp soy sauce.
2 Peel and finely shred a 1cm/½in piece of fresh root ginger and add it to the mixture with 1 finely shredded spring onion (scallion). Stir well to mix.

Nuoc Cham sauce

This rich red sauce is traditionally served with spring rolls. Its hot, sweet and sour flavours work well with meat, fish and vegetable fillings.

1 Remove the seeds from 2 fresh red chillies and pound them to a paste with 2 garlic cloves using a mortar and pestle.
2 Scrape the pounded chilli and garlic into a small bowl and add 15ml/1 tbsp caster (superfine) sugar, 45ml/3 tbsp fish sauce and lime juice to taste. Stir well to mix. Chill until needed.

Tomato and chilli simple salsa

This is delicious in all kinds of wraps, or served as an accompaniment.

1 To make, peel, and seed 3 large tomatoes. Chop them and put them in a bowl with the juice of 1 lime.
2 Add to the bowl

some chopped fresh coriander (cilantro), 1 chopped onion and 3 chillies, seeded and chopped. Mix, season with salt and set aside for 15 minutes before serving.

Apricot and amaretto sauce

This sauce goes well with sweet wraps containing fruit and ice cream.

1 Drain a can of apricots, reserving 30ml/2 tbsp of the juice. Pour this into a blender, add the apricots and purée.
2 Stir in 15–30ml/1–2 tbsp Amaretto liqueur then serve with the filled wrap.

Fabulous ways with fillings and sauces

Snacks and appetizers

At first glance, wraps seem fairly substantial, but they can make some of the most stunning snacks and appetizers.

The trick is to use small wrappers, such as vine leaves, aubergine (eggplant) slices or small tortillas, or cut larger tortilla rolls into short bitesize lengths. Turn them on their sides to reveal the attractive layering of the filling.

Spring rolls make excellent hot snacks, and are surprisingly easy to make. They are also hugely versatile and can be filled with a whole range of ingredients – from vegetarian options such as fried tofu and mushrooms to prawns (shrimp) or thinly sliced pork. They are delicious eaten as soon as they are made, especially when dipped into a sweet and spicy sauce. For contrast, serve elegant Vietnamese rice paper rolls. Their transparent wrappers display the tempting fillings within, making them irresistible party offerings.

Also excellent for handing round are individual dolmades made with vine leaves. The traditional Greek filling is a simple herb and rice combination, but for special occasions why not fill them with a delicately-flavoured mixture of lightly poached red mullet with pine nuts.

If you fancy something sweet, try rolling slices of panettone around a rich filling of mascarpone and crushed berries. This is much easier than it sounds, and makes a delectable dessert or mid-morning treat.

California wrap

The classic California sushi roll combines crab meat and avocado with vinegared rice in a sheet of thin, dried seaweed, and involves the use of a bamboo mat. This recipe takes the easy track, and simply encloses the filling in a tortilla wrap.

Serves four

1 ripe avocado, halved, stoned (pitted) and peeled
15ml/1 tbsp mayonnaise
275g/10oz crab meat
2 spring onions (scallions), chopped
4 large wheat flour tortillas or tortilla wraps
4 sheets nori seaweed
wasabi paste (optional)
sprigs of fresh coriander (cilantro), to garnish

For the vinegared rice

200g/7oz/1 cup Japanese short grain rice
20ml/4 tsp sugar
5ml/1 tsp salt
40ml/8 tsp rice vinegar

1 Make the vinegared rice. Rinse the rice in a sieve under cold running water until the water runs clear. Leave in the sieve and drain for 1 hour, then put it in a heavy pan. Pour in 250ml/8fl oz/1 cup water, cover and bring to the boil. Lower the heat and simmer for 12 minutes without lifting the lid. Remove from the heat and leave for 10 minutes.

2 Spoon the rice into a large bowl. Dissolve the sugar and salt in the rice vinegar, then fold the mixture into the hot rice, using a wooden spoon or wet fish slice (metal spatula). Cover the bowl and leave to cool. Meanwhile, mash the avocado together with the mayonnaise, then fold in the crab meat and chopped spring onions.

3 Lay a tortilla flat and cover it with a sheet of nori seaweed, cut to fit. Spread with a layer of the rice. Using the tip of your finger, dot wasabi paste (if using) very lightly down the centre of the rice. Spread one-quarter of the avocado mixture on top.

4 Roll up the tortilla into a cigar shape, pressing down gently as you do so, to compress the rice a little. Make three more rolls in the same way.

5 Serve the rolls simply, by wrapping their lower halves in paper, and hold in the hand to eat. For a special occasion, slice the rolls in half diagonally, and place two pieces on each plate. Garnish with a few sprigs of coriander.

Cook's tip
Take care when using wasabi paste. This Japanese green seasoning packs a punch that is like very hot mustard.

Tortilla cones with smoked salmon and soft cheese

Whether you're snuggling up on the sofa to watch a late night movie or catering for a crowd, these simple yet sophisticated wraps are irresistible.

Serves four

115g/4oz/½ cup soft white (farmer's) cheese
30ml/2 tbsp roughly chopped fresh dill
juice of 1 lemon
1 small red onion
15ml/1 tbsp drained bottled capers
30ml/2 tbsp extra virgin olive oil
30ml/2 tbsp roughly chopped fresh flat leaf parsley
115g/4oz smoked salmon
8 small or 4 large wheat flour tortillas
salt and ground black pepper
lemon wedges, for squeezing

Variation
Tortilla cones make versatile vehicles for all kinds of fillings. Try soft cheese with red pesto and chopped sun-dried tomatoes, or mackerel pâté with slices of cucumber.

1 Place the soft cheese in a small bowl and mix in half the chopped dill. Add a little salt and pepper and just a dash of the lemon juice to taste. Reserve the remaining lemon juice in a separate mixing bowl.

2 Finely chop the red onion. Add the onion, capers and olive oil to the lemon juice. Add the chopped flat leaf parsley and the remaining dill and gently stir.

3 Cut the smoked salmon into short, thin strips, and add to the red onion mixture. Toss to mix. Season to taste with plenty of pepper.

4 If using small tortillas, leave them whole, but large ones need to be cut in half. Spread a little of the soft cheese mixture on each piece of tortilla and top with the smoked salmon mixture.

5 Roll up the tortillas into cones and secure with wooden cocktail sticks (toothpicks). Arrange on a serving plate and add some lemon wedges, for squeezing. Serve immediately.

Cook's tip
You can also use salted capers in this dish but rinse them thoroughly under cold running water before using.

Crispy Shanghai spring rolls

Surprisingly simple to make, spring rolls always go down well and are deliciously dippable. In this version, tofu, pork and prawns are teamed with crunchy stir-fried vegetables.

Serves four

12 spring roll wrappers, thawed if frozen
30ml/2 tbsp plain (all-purpose) flour mixed to a paste with water
oil for deep-frying

For the filling

6 Chinese dried mushrooms, soaked for 30 minutes in warm water
150g/5oz firm tofu
30ml/2 tbsp sunflower oil
225g/8oz/1 cup minced (ground) pork
225g/8oz peeled cooked prawns (shrimp), roughly chopped
2.5ml/½ tsp cornflour (cornstarch) mixed to a paste with 15ml/1 tbsp soy sauce
75g/3oz/½ cup each grated carrot, sliced water chestnuts and beansprouts
6 spring onions (scallions), finely chopped
2.5ml/½ tsp sesame oil

For the dipping sauce

105ml/7 tbsp light soy sauce
15ml/1 tbsp sweet chilli sauce
rice vinegar, to taste

1 Make the filling. Drain the mushrooms. Discard the stems and chop the caps finely. Chop the tofu. Heat the oil in a wok and stir-fry the pork for about 3 minutes until the colour changes. Add the prawns, cornflour paste and grated carrot. Stir in the water chestnuts.

2 Add the beansprouts and spring onions and toss over a high heat for 1 minute. Add the mushrooms and tofu and toss to mix. Tip into a large shallow dish and add the sesame oil. Toss again, then spread out evenly to cool quickly. Make the dipping sauce by mixing all the ingredients in a bowl.

3 Peel off one of the spring roll wrappers, using a metal spatula if necessary, and keep the remaining wrappers moist under a damp cloth. Place the wrapper on a board, with a corner facing you.

4 Spoon some of the filling in the centre, and fold the nearest corner to you over it. Smear a little flour paste on the sides, turn them to the middle, envelope fashion, and roll up. Use a little more paste to seal the join. Make more rolls in the same way.

5 Heat the oil for deep-frying to 190°C/375°F or until a cube of bread added to the oil browns in about 45 seconds. Deep-fry the spring rolls in batches for 3 minutes, or until they are crisp and golden. Drain on kitchen paper and serve immediately with the dipping sauce.

> **Cook's tip**
> Stir-fried chicken would also work well in a spring roll. Try a mixture of chicken, spring onions (scallions), water chestnuts and mushrooms.

Vietnamese rice paper rolls

Assemble your own filled pancakes, mixing tasty ingredients such as vermicelli, fresh herbs and tender pork. Finish by dipping them in a spicy black bean sauce.

Serves eight

1 small onion, sliced
a few fresh coriander (cilantro) stems
30ml/2 tbsp fish sauce
225g/8oz piece belly pork, boned and rind removed
250g/9oz fine rice vermicelli
225g/8oz/1 cup beansprouts, rinsed and drained
8 crisp lettuce leaves, halved
fresh mint and coriander (cilantro) leaves
175g/6oz peeled cooked prawns (shrimp)
16 large rice paper pancakes

For the black bean sauce

15–30ml/1–2 tbsp groundnut (peanut) oil
2 garlic cloves, crushed
1 fresh red chilli, seeded and sliced
60ml/4 tbsp canned salted black beans
30ml/2 tbsp fish sauce
5ml/1 tsp rice vinegar
10–15ml/2–3 tsp soft light brown sugar
15ml/1 tbsp crunchy peanut butter
15ml/1 tbsp sesame seeds, dry-fried
5ml/1 tsp sesame oil
90ml/6 tbsp chicken stock

1 Mix the onion slices, coriander stems and fish sauce in a large pan. Pour in 2 litres/3½ pints/8 cups water. Bring to the boil, add the pork and boil for 20–30 minutes, turning the meat occasionally until it is tender when tested with a skewer. Lift the pork out of the pan, leave to cool, then slice into thin strips.

2 Make the sauce. Heat the oil in a frying pan and fry the garlic and chilli for 1 minute. Stir in all the remaining ingredients, mix well, then tip into a food processor and process briefly. The sauce should remain fairly chunky. Pour into a pan and keep warm over a low heat.

3 Soak the rice vermicelli in warm water until softened. Drain well, then snip or slice into neat lengths. Bring a pan of water to the boil and add the vermicelli. As soon as the water boils again, drain the noodles, rinse them under cold water, then drain them again and tip into a bowl.

4 Put the beansprouts on a separate dish, and arrange the lettuce and herb leaves on a large platter. Put the prawns in a bowl.

5 When almost ready to serve, place the rice paper pancakes two at a time on a dishtowel and brush both sides with warm water to soften them. Carefully transfer two pancakes to each serving plate.

6 Each guest places half a lettuce leaf on one end of a pancake, topping it with noodles and beansprouts, a few fresh herb leaves and strips of cooked pork. The pancake is rolled around the filling once, then prawns are placed on the open part and the pancake is finally rolled up completely. The second pancake is filled in the same way. The warm black bean sauce is served in a bowl for dipping.

Cook's tip
Take care when rolling the delicate rice paper, as it can easily tear.

Red mullet dolmades

The fish stays beautifully moist in these elegant stuffed vine leaves. They make a tasty and sophisticated first course when served with the orange butter sauce. Alternatively, serve them as finger food, with the sauce as a dip.

Serves four

8 preserved vine leaves
225g/8oz red mullet fillets, scaled
45ml/3 tbsp dry white wine
115g/4oz/1 cup cooked long grain rice
25g/1oz/$\frac{1}{3}$ cup pine nuts
45ml/3 tbsp chopped fresh parsley
grated rind and juice of 1 lemon
salt and ground black pepper

For the orange butter sauce
grated rind and juice of 2 oranges
2 shallots, very finely chopped
25g/1oz/2 tbsp chilled butter, diced

Variation
Red mullet has a robust and distinctive flavour, which goes especially well with the orange sauce, but snapper, plaice or flounder make good substitutes.

1 Preheat the oven to 200°C/400°F/Gas 6. Rinse the vine leaves in plenty of cold water. Put in a bowl, cover with boiling water and leave for 10 minutes. Drain the leaves thoroughly.

2 Put the red mullet fillets in a shallow pan and season with salt and pepper. Pour over the wine, bring to the boil, then lower the heat and poach the fish gently for about 3 minutes until just cooked. Strain, reserving the cooking liquid.

3 Remove the skin from the fish fillets and flake the flesh into a bowl. Add the cooked rice, pine nuts, chopped parsley, lemon rind and juice and stir gently to mix through. Season to taste with salt and pepper.

4 Place a vine leaf, veined side up, on a board and cut off any stalk. Place a heaped teaspoonful of the rice mixture near the stalk end. Fold that end over the filling, then fold in the sides. Carefully roll the leaf up into a neat cigar shape. Make seven more dolmades in the same way.

5 Arrange the dolmades in a baking dish, with the joins underneath. Pour over the reserved cooking liquid, cover and place the dolmades in the oven for 8 minutes, or until they are heated through.

6 Make the sauce by mixing the orange rind and juice with the shallots in a pan. Bring to the boil and boil vigorously for about 4 minutes until the mixture is reduced and syrupy. Strain into a clean pan, discarding the shallots. Beat in the butter, a piece at a time. Reheat gently, but do not let the sauce boil.

7 Using a slotted spoon, transfer the dolmades to a serving dish, pour over the sauce and serve.

Aubergine, tomato and mozzarella wraps

Robust vegetables such as aubergines make ideal wraps. Next time you are looking for something a little out of the ordinary, try these rich and flavourful parcels.

Serves four

2 large, long aubergines (eggplant)
225g/8oz mozzarella cheese
2 plum tomatoes
16 large fresh basil leaves
30ml/2 tbsp extra virgin olive oil
salt and ground black pepper
toasted pine nuts and torn fresh basil leaves, to garnish

For the dressing

60ml/4 tbsp extra virgin olive oil
5ml/1 tsp balsamic vinegar
15ml/1 tbsp sun-dried tomato paste
15ml/1 tbsp lemon juice

Variation

Vine-ripened tomatoes are best for this dish. If not available, however, try smoked sun-dried tomatoes in oil or substitute pimientos, heart-shaped, sweet red (bell) peppers, which are usually available bottled.

1 Cut each aubergine lengthways into eight thin slices, about 5mm/¼in thick. Bring a large pan of water to the boil, add the slices and cook for 2 minutes, until softened. Drain in a colander, then pat dry with kitchen paper.

2 Cut the mozzarella cheese into eight slices. Trim the top and base of each tomato, then slice each into eight slices.

3 Lay an aubergine slice on a chopping board and place another slice on top of it so that they form a cross. Place a slice of tomato in the centre, season with salt and pepper, then add a basil leaf followed by a slice of mozzarella, another basil leaf, a slice of tomato and a little more seasoning, if you like.

4 Bring up the ends of the aubergine slices around the filling to make a neat parcel. Repeat with the remaining ingredients to make another seven parcels. Cover with clear film (plastic wrap) and chill for at least 20 minutes.

5 Meanwhile, make the dressing by whisking all the ingredients together in a small bowl. Brush the parcels with the olive oil and grill (broil) under a medium heat for about 5 minutes on each side, or until golden. Serve hot, sprinkled with the toasted pine nuts and basil leaves. Offer the dressing separately.

Cook's tip
To toast the pine nuts, spread them out in a grill (broiler) tray and place under a medium grill for 3–4 minutes, shaking the tray often so that they brown all over. Watch them closely, so that they do not burn.

Panettone rolls with mascarpone and crushed berries

A rich yeasted bread from Italy, panettone is packed with dried fruit and candied peel. It makes a superb sweet wrap, especially if you team it with soft, creamy cheese and tart fruit.

Serves four

4 x 1cm/½in panettone slices, cut from a 500g/1¼lb loaf
90–120ml/6–8 tbsp mascarpone or cream cheese
16–20 mixed berries, such as blackberries, youngberries and raspberries
icing (confectioners') sugar, to serve
sprigs of redcurrants or blackcurrants, to decorate and serve

Variations
- Use raisin bread or any other fruit bread instead of panettone. Cut off the crusts before flattening the slices.
- Try topping the mascarpone or cream cheese with poached dried apricots.

1 Place a slice of panettone between two sheets of clear film (plastic wrap). Have the longer side facing you. Using a rolling pin, roll the bread lightly and evenly, so that it flattens to about half its original thickness, and becomes broader, not longer.

2 Lift off the top piece of clear film. Spread the panettone thickly with the mascarpone or cream cheese, top with four or five berries, and squash each berry lightly with a fork.

3 Using the clear film as a guide, roll up the bread, Swiss-roll (jelly-roll) fashion, press gently to fix the shape, then cut into three equal pieces.

4 Use the remaining panettone, mascarpone and berries to make more rolls in the same way.

5 Place the rolls on a flat board or plate, arranging them so that the filling is visible. Dust generously with icing sugar and decorate with sprigs of redcurrants or blackcurrants.

Cook's tips
These make the perfect dinner party dessert, much easier to manage than one that needs to be spooned into bowls – and much less to wash up afterwards. Serve them with small cups of strong coffee.

Lunchtime wraps

"It's a wrap" is the cry that goes up when a movie scene has been shot successfully, so what better way to celebrate a good morning's work (or play) than with a delectable light lunch, presented in its own edible parcel? The emphasis here is on easy eating, and draws on the flavours and colours of cuisines from around the world. Try offerings such as roasted vegetables wrapped in Middle Eastern flat bread or a Mediterranean-inspired tortilla roll filled with caramelized onions, pancetta and mozzarella cheese.

A freshly made omelette makes a very good wrap, either on its own or inside a thin tortilla. Try teaming it with a medley of Asian vegetables, such as broccoli, pak choi (bok choy) and beansprouts, though it will still taste delicious (although perhaps not so authentic) with whatever combination of vegetables you can find in the refrigerator.

Of course, no collection of lunchtime wraps would be complete without a few examples from Mexico, the birthplace of the tortilla wrap. In this chapter mouthwatering chicken chimichangas and red snapper burritos share the limelight with beef enchiladas in a spicy chilli sauce. Each one is full of flavour and sure to leave you satisfied.

Not remotely Mexican, but utterly irresistible all the same, are the cooked apples in tortilla wraps, smothered in rich butterscotch sauce. If you've never had a sweet tortilla, prepare to be converted.

Roasted vegetable lavash wrap

Middle Eastern flat breads are perfect for casual wraps. Supply fragrant roasted vegetables and invite guests to tear off suitably sized pieces and wrap, fold or roll them as they wish.

Serves four

3 courgettes (zucchini), trimmed and sliced lengthways
1 large fennel bulb, cut into wedges
450g/1lb butternut squash, seeded and cut into 2cm/¾in chunks
12 shallots
2 red (bell) peppers, seeded and cut lengthways into thick slices
4 plum tomatoes, halved and seeded
45ml/3 tbsp extra virgin olive oil
2 garlic cloves, crushed
5ml/1 tsp balsamic vinegar
salt and ground black pepper

To serve

lavash or other flat bread
fresh or good quality bottled pesto
chopped fresh mint
Greek (US strained plain) yogurt
feta cheese, cubed

1 Preheat the oven to 220°C/425°F/Gas 7. Place the courgettes, fennel, butternut squash, shallots, peppers and tomatoes in a large bowl. Add the olive oil, garlic and balsamic vinegar and toss until all the ingredients are thoroughly coated in the mixture. Set aside for about 10 minutes to allow the flavours to mingle.

2 Using a slotted spoon, lift just the tomatoes and butternut squash out of the mixture and set them aside on a plate. Use the spoon to transfer all the remaining vegetables to a large roasting pan. Brush with half the oil and vinegar mixture remaining in the bowl, season and roast for 25 minutes.

3 Remove the pan from the oven and turn the vegetables over. Brush with the rest of the oil and vinegar mixture, add the squash and tomatoes and cook for a further 20–25 minutes or until all the vegetables are tender and have begun to char around the edges.

4 Put the bread on the table, with the pesto, mint, yogurt and feta cheese in separate bowls. Spoon the roasted vegetables on to a large platter and invite everyone to tuck in.

Cook's tip
Thin and malleable, lavash makes the ideal wrap. The bread is often very large, up to 60cm/2ft in diameter, but is easily torn into more manageable pieces for filling and rolling.

Tomato tortillas with pancetta and caramelized red onions

Imagine crisp frazzled pancetta teamed with red onions, strips of sun-dried tomato and melting mozzarella cheese in a spicy tomato tortilla – delicious. Lunch time is always the right time for something as tempting as this.

Serves four

12 pieces of sun-dried tomato in oil, plus 30ml/2 tbsp oil from the jar
4 red onions, about 500g/1¼lb
130g/4½oz cubed dry-cured pancetta
4 spicy tomato tortilla wraps or regular wheat flour tortillas
115g/4oz mozzarella cheese
fresh basil leaves, to garnish

Variation
Anchovies and caramelized onions are another classic combination. Tear six drained canned anchovy fillets into shreds and add them to the onions in step 3 instead of the pancetta.

1 Heat the oil from the jar of sun-dried tomatoes in a large frying pan. Halve and thinly slice the red onions. Add them to the pan and fry, stirring occasionally, for 5 minutes until softened.

2 Cut the sun-dried tomatoes into strips and add them to the pan. Reduce the heat to low and cook for 15–20 minutes more, stirring occasionally until the onions have begun to caramelize.

3 Grill (broil) the pancetta until crisp, turning over halfway through cooking. Set aside but leave the grill (broiler) on. Gently warm the tortilla wraps or wheat tortillas under the grill, as directed on the package. Cut the mozzarella cheese into thick slices.

4 Top each wrap or tortilla in turn with one-quarter of the onion mixture, placing it in a band across the centre. Add one-quarter of the pancetta and top with a few mozzarella slices.

5 Carefully transfer the tortillas to the grill and cook for just long enough to melt the cheese. Fold the exposed pieces of tortilla over to make a simple wrap. Garnish with the fresh basil leaves and serve immediately.

Cook's tip
Pancetta is a dry-cured Italian ham and is available pre-cubed at most large stores and supermarkets. Diced bacon can be used instead.

Coriander omelette wraps with stir-fried vegetables

Good to look at and good for you too – that describes these tasty wraps, which are packed with healthy vegetables. This is a great recipe for impromptu lunches, as the stir-fry can be varied to suit whatever ingredients you have.

Serves four

150g/5oz broccoli, cut into small florets
30ml/2 tbsp groundnut (peanut) oil
1cm/½in piece of fresh root ginger, finely grated
1 large garlic clove, crushed
2 fresh red chillies, seeded and finely sliced
4 spring onions (scallions), sliced diagonally
175g/6oz/3 cups shredded pak choi (bok choy)
50g/2oz/2 cups fresh coriander (cilantro) leaves, plus extra to garnish
115g/4oz/½ cup beansprouts
45ml/3 tbsp black bean sauce
4 eggs
salt and ground black pepper

1 Blanch the broccoli in salted boiling water for 2 minutes. Drain, then refresh under cold water and drain again.

2 Meanwhile, heat 15ml/1 tbsp of the oil in a large frying pan or wok. Stir-fry the ginger, garlic and half the chilli for 1 minute, then add the spring onions, broccoli and pak choi. Using two wooden spatulas, toss the ingredients over the heat for 2 minutes.

3 Chop three-quarters of the coriander and add to the pan or wok, with the beansprouts. Stir-fry for 1 minute, then add the black bean sauce and heat through for 1 minute more. Remove the pan from the heat and keep warm.

4 Break up the eggs lightly with a fork and season well. Heat a little of the remaining oil in a small frying pan and add one-quarter of the beaten egg.

5 Swirl the pan so the egg spreads to cover the base, then sprinkle over one-quarter of the reserved coriander leaves. Cook until just set, then turn out the omelette on to a plate and keep warm while you make three more omelettes, adding more oil when necessary.

6 Spoon the vegetable stir-fry on to the omelettes and gently roll up. Cut in half crossways and serve on individual plates, garnished with the extra coriander leaves and the remaining chilli.

Chicken and tomatillo chimichangas

These fried burritos are a favourite street food in Mexico, where tomatillos are widely cultivated. Despite the name, this fruit is related to physalis, and has a tart flavour, with a hint of lemon.

Serves four

2 skinless chicken breast fillets
1 chipotle chilli
15ml/1 tbsp vegetable oil
2 onions, finely chopped
4 garlic cloves, crushed
2.5ml/½ tsp ground cumin
2.5ml/½ tsp ground coriander
2.5ml/½ tsp ground cinnamon
2.5ml/½ tsp ground cloves
300g/11oz/scant 2 cups drained canned tomatillos
400g/14oz/2⅓ cups drained canned pinto beans
8 large wheat flour tortillas
oil, for frying
salt and ground black pepper

Variation
Tomatillos have a unique flavour, so there's no real substitute. If you want, however, chopped vine-ripened tomatoes can be used instead.

1 Put the chicken breast fillets in a large pan, pour over water to cover and add the chilli. Bring to the boil, lower the heat and simmer for 10 minutes, or until the chicken is cooked through and the chilli has softened.

2 Remove the chilli and chop it finely with a small, sharp knife. Discard the seeds. Lift the chicken fillets out of the pan and put them on a chopping board. Leave to cool slightly, then shred with two forks.

3 Heat the oil in a frying pan. Add the onions and cook, stirring occasionally, until soft and translucent, then add the garlic and ground spices and cook for about 3 minutes more.

4 Add the tomatillos and pinto beans to the pan. Cook over a medium heat for 5 minutes, stirring constantly to break up the tomatillos and some of the beans. Simmer for 5 minutes more, then add the chicken and seasoning.

5 Warm the tortillas, following the instructions on the package. Spoon one-eighth of the filling into the centre of a tortilla, fold in both sides, then fold the bottom of the tortilla up and the top down to form a neat burrito. Secure with a cocktail stick (toothpick), if necessary.

6 Heat the oil in a large frying pan and fry the chimichangas in batches until crisp, turning once. Remove them from the oil with a fish slice (metal spatula) and drain on kitchen paper. Serve hot.

Beef enchiladas with red sauce and mango salsa

Chillies and tender braised steak make a spicy filling for these hearty tortillas. Mango salsa is the ideal accompaniment.

Serves three

500g/1¼lb rump (round) steak, cut into 5cm/2in cubes
2 ancho chillies, seeded
2 pasilla chillies, seeded
30ml/2 tbsp sunflower oil
2 garlic cloves, crushed
10ml/2 tsp dried oregano
2.5ml/½ tsp ground cumin
7 fresh corn tortillas
shredded onion and flat leaf parsley, to garnish

For the mango salsa

2 fresh mild red chillies
2 ripe mangoes, peeled and diced
1 white onion, chopped
small bunch of fresh coriander (cilantro), chopped
grated rind and juice of 1 lime

Variation
Use wheat flour tortillas if you can't locate corn ones, but ensure that you heat them slightly before filling and rolling, otherwise they will crack as you roll them.

1 Make the mango salsa. Grill (broil) the chillies until the skins are charred. Place in a bowl, cover with clear film (plastic wrap) and leave for 20 minutes.

2 Meanwhile, put the diced mango in a bowl and add the chopped onion and coriander. Rub the skins off the chillies, then slit them and remove the seeds. Chop the flesh and add it to the bowl with the lime rind and juice. Cover and chill for at least 1 hour before serving.

3 Put the steak in a deep frying pan with water to cover. Bring to the boil, then simmer for 1–1½ hours. Put the ancho and pasilla chillies in a bowl and pour over hot water to cover. Leave to soak for 30 minutes, then transfer to a blender and whiz to a smooth paste.

4 Drain the steak well and let it cool, reserving 250ml/8fl oz/1 cup of the cooking liquid. Heat the oil in the clean frying pan and fry the garlic, oregano and cumin for 2 minutes. Stir in the chilli paste and the reserved cooking liquid. Tear one of the tortillas into small pieces and add it to the mixture.

5 Bring to the boil, then lower the heat. Simmer for 10 minutes, stirring occasionally, until the sauce has thickened.

6 Shred the steak, using two forks, and stir it into the sauce. Heat through for a few minutes. Spoon some of the meat mixture on to a tortilla and roll it up to make an enchilada. Place on a serving platter and keep warm until you have filled and rolled all the tortillas. Garnish with onion shreds and flat leaf parsley and serve with the mango salsa.

Cook's tip
Take great care when handling chillies, as the compound *capsaicin* that they contain is a powerful irritant. Wear gloves if possible or wash your hands in soapy water after touching them.

Red snapper burritos

Open these tortilla envelopes to reveal the delectable filling of tender red snapper with rice, chillies, almonds, tomatoes, and melted Monterey Jack cheese.

Serves four

3 red snapper fillets or grey mullet, John Dory or sea bass
90g/3½oz/½ cup long grain rice
30ml/2 tbsp sunflower oil
1 small onion, finely chopped
5ml/1 tsp ground achiote seed (annatto powder)
1 pasilla or similar dried chilli, seeded and ground
75g/3oz/¾ cup slivered almonds
200g/7oz can chopped tomatoes in tomato juice
150g/5oz/1¼ cups grated Monterey Jack or mild Cheddar cheese
8 large wheat flour tortillas
fresh flat leaf parsley, spring onions (scallions), sliced diagonally, and lime wedges, to garnish

1 Grill (broil) the fish on a lightly oiled rack for about 5 minutes, turning over once. When completely cool, remove the skin and flake the fish into a bowl. Set it aside.

2 Meanwhile, put the rice in a pan, cover with cold water, put a lid on the pan and bring to the boil. Drain, rinse under plenty of cold running water and drain again.

3 Heat the oil in a pan, add the onion and fry until soft and translucent. Stir in the ground achiote and the chilli and cook for 5 minutes.

4 Add the rice, stir well, then stir in the flaked fish and slivered almonds. Add the tomatoes, with their juices. Cook over a medium heat until the juice has been absorbed and the rice is tender. Stir in the grated cheese and remove the pan from the heat. Warm the tortillas as directed on the package.

5 Spoon one-eighth of the filling into the centre of a tortilla, fold in both sides, then fold the bottom of the tortilla up and the top down to form a burrito. Place folded side down on a plate and keep warm while you fill and shape the remaining burritos in the same way. Garnish with the parsley, spring onions and lime wedges.

Cook's tip
Achiote is a ground spice that is popular in Mexico. It comes from the red-orange seeds of the annatto tree, and gives food a distinctive, earthy flavour. It isn't essential to this recipe, so if you can't locate it, just leave it out.

Apple wraps with butterscotch sauce

Tortillas don't have to be savoury. Add the right filling and they make marvellous sweet treats, especially if you use thin wraps rather than the traditional thick tortillas.

Serves four

4 plain tortilla wraps
4 eating apples
90g/3½oz/scant ½ cup butter
225g/8oz/1 cup light muscovado (brown) sugar
150ml/¼ pint/⅔ cup double (heavy) cream

Variations
- You can also use pears, peaches or fresh apricots instead of apples.
- Serve with a little yogurt or crème fraîche if you like.

1 Preheat the oven to 200°C/400°F/Gas 6. Wrap the tortillas in foil and place them on a baking sheet. Heat in the oven for 8 minutes.

2 Meanwhile, core but do not peel the apples. Cut them in eighths. Heat 15g/½oz/1 tbsp of the butter in a large heavy frying pan. Add the apples and cook over a medium heat until golden on both sides. Using a slotted spoon, transfer the apples to a bowl, cover with foil and keep warm in the oven.

3 Add the remainder of the butter to the pan. Once it has melted, add the muscovado sugar. When it has dissolved and the mixture is bubbling, stir in the cream. Continue cooking until it forms a smooth butterscotch sauce.

4 Unwrap the tortillas and place one on each plate. Put a spoonful of the apple pieces on each one and make a fajita by bringing up the bottom and folding in the sides. Secure them with a wooden cocktail stick (toothpick) if necessary.

5 Spoon more apples into the wrap so that they spill out and on to the plate. Drizzle a little of the butterscotch sauce over the apple filling and serve at once. Offer the remaining butterscotch sauce separately.

Cook's tip
There's no delicate way to eat these wickedly rich treats, but that's part of the enjoyment. Use a spoon and fork to spear the apples and tear the tortillas, and supply paper napkins to catch any drips.

Gourmet wraps

Just to prove that wraps aren't exclusively something you throw together in seconds when you are starving hungry, here are some sophisticated dishes for special occasions. Peking duck is a favourite choice for diners at Chinese restaurants, though there is always the risk of not being served enough pancakes. Making your own at home solves this problem. This recipe does require a bit of forward planning but the effort is worth it.

Another dish whose origins lie in Asian cooking are parcels of sticky rice and chicken in an exotic lotus leaf wrapping. These leaves look wonderful, and are ideal for enclosing food – don't forget to remind guests they aren't edible, however.

For some Moroccan flavour, sample the lamb kebab wraps with lightly spiced courgettes (zucchini). Stylish but simple, these wraps are great for easy entertaining and would make the perfect meal when dining *al fresco*. Cook the kebabs over the barbecue and let the wafting aromas of the cooking food do the rest.

Seafood is always a popular choice when entertaining, and it teams well with a variety of wraps, such as lettuce leaves and nori seaweed. Here, sole is lightly steamed in individual lettuce parcels, and another recipe shows you how to prepare the ingredients necessary for making your own delightful hand-rolled sushi.

For a light but elegant dessert, try scoops of cranberry sorbet in lace pancakes, or wrap up the meal with coffee crêpes filled with peaches and amaretto cream. Both of these are not difficult to make, and look stunning.

Lamb kebab wraps with Moroccan spiced courgettes

A mixture of bulgur wheat and spiced lamb makes for delicious kebabs, which taste even better when tucked into tortillas with a spoonful of courgettes.

Serves four

40g/1½oz/¼ cup bulgur wheat
450g/1lb/2 cups minced (ground) lamb
1 egg yolk
1 garlic clove, crushed
30ml/2 tbsp finely chopped fresh parsley, plus extra leaves to garnish
5ml/1 tsp paprika
2.5ml/½ tsp ras el hanout or 1.5ml/¼ tsp chilli powder
30ml/2 tbsp blanched almonds, chopped
8 wheat flour tortillas or tortilla wraps
salt and ground black pepper

For the spiced courgettes
225g/8oz small courgettes (zucchini)
30ml/2 tbsp extra virgin olive oil, plus extra for greasing
30ml/2 tbsp chopped fresh parsley
small red onion, finely chopped
1 garlic clove, crushed
1.5ml/¼ tsp crushed chillies
1.5ml/¼ tsp paprika
1.5ml/¼ tsp ground cumin

1 Place the bulgur wheat in a large bowl and pour over enough boiling water to cover generously. Leave to soak for about 20 minutes. Place eight bamboo skewers in a bowl of cold water and leave to soak.

2 Preheat the oven to 190°C/375°F/Gas 5. Line a small sieve with a clean dishtowel. Scald the towel by pouring boiling water through it, then place the lined sieve in the sink and carefully pour in the bulgur wheat. When most of the liquid has drained, gather up the sides of the dishtowel and squeeze tightly to extract as much liquid as possible.

3 Tip the bulgur wheat into a bowl and add the lamb and egg yolk. Mix well, then add the garlic, parsley, spices, almonds and salt and pepper. Work together with your hands until well combined, then remove from the bowl and roll into a rough sausage shape. Cut into 16 pieces and roll each piece to a flat oval patty. Push two patties on to each drained skewer.

4 Make the spiced courgettes. Cut the courgettes into short batons and place in a lightly oiled baking dish. Mix together the parsley, onion, garlic, spices and oil and season with salt. Pour this mixture over the courgettes and toss gently. Cover with foil and bake for 10 minutes.

5 Preheat the grill (broiler). Wrap the tortillas in foil and place them on a baking sheet. Put them in the oven to heat. At the same time, baste the courgettes. Grill (broil) the lamb kebabs for 3–4 minutes on each side, until they are just starting to char on the outside but are beautifully tender inside.

6 Test the courgettes. They should be just tender. Unwrap the tortillas and place them on individual plates. Spoon a little of the courgette mixture on to each one, add a kebab and roll up. Garnish with extra parsley and serve immediately.

Peking duck with mandarin pancakes

You need to start this recipe a couple of days ahead, but the end result is worth it – delectable duck in wafer-thin wraps spread with sauce and crisp cucumber and spring onions.

Serves eight

1 duck, about 2.25kg/5lb
45ml/3 tbsp clear honey
5ml/1 tsp salt
1 bunch spring onions (scallions), cut into strips
1 cucumber, seeded and cut into thin strips

For the mandarin pancakes
275g/10oz/2½ cups strong white bread flour
5ml/1 tsp salt
45ml/3 tbsp groundnut (peanut) oil

For the dipping sauces
120ml/4fl oz/½ cup hoisin sauce
120ml/4fl oz/½ cup plum sauce

Variation
This is the traditional recipe but, if short of time, you can use 1 skinless duck breast portion for every 2 people instead of the whole duck. Add to the marinade in step 2 and leave for at least 2 hours.

1 Bring a large pan of water to the boil. Place the duck on a trivet in the sink and pour the boiling water over it. Lift the duck out on the trivet and drain. Tie kitchen string around the legs of the bird and suspend it from a butcher's hook in a cool place. Place a bowl underneath and leave overnight.

2 The next day, mix the honey and salt with 30ml/2 tbsp water. Brush half the mixture over the duck skin. Hang the bird up again and leave for 2–3 hours. Repeat and leave for 3–4 hours.

3 Make the pancakes. Sift the flour and salt into a bowl. Add one-third of the oil, then add 250ml/8fl oz/1 cup boiling water to form a soft dough. Knead for 3 minutes by hand. Rest for 30 minutes.

4 Preheat the oven to 230°C/450°F/Gas 8. Knead the dough, then divide it into 24 pieces and roll each piece to a 15cm/6in round. Brush the surface of half the rounds with oil, then sandwich the rounds together. Oil two frying pans. Add one pancake pair to each pan and cook for 3 minutes. Turn over and cook for 3 minutes more.

5 Pull the double pancakes apart. Stack on a plate, with baking parchment between them. Continue until all the pancakes have been cooked. When cool, wrap them tightly in foil and set aside.

6 Put the duck on a rack in a roasting pan and place it in the oven. Reduce the temperature to 180°C/350°F/Gas 4 and roast the duck for 1¾ hours without basting. Check that the skin is crisp. If not, increase the oven temperature and roast for 15 minutes more.

7 Meanwhile, place the spring onion strips in iced water to crisp up. Drain. Pat the pieces of cucumber dry on kitchen paper. Reheat the pancakes by steaming the foil parcel for 5–10 minutes in a bamboo steamer over a wok of boiling water. Pour the dipping sauces into individual dishes.

8 Carve the duck into 4cm/1½in pieces. At the table, each guest smears some of the prepared sauce on a pancake, tops
it with a small amount of crisp duck skin and meat, and adds cucumber and spring onion strips before rolling up the pancake and eating it.

Tamales filled with spiced pork

Corn husk parcels filled with pork and chilli masa dough make an impressive centrepiece for a special occasion.

Serves six

500g/1¼lb lean pork, cut into 5cm/2in cubes
750ml/1¼ pints/3 cups chicken stock
600g/1lb 6oz/4½ cups masa harina
450g/1lb/2½ cups lard or white cooking fat, softened
30ml/2 tbsp salt
12 large dried corn husks
2 ancho chillies, seeded
15ml/1 tbsp vegetable oil
1 onion, finely chopped
2–3 garlic cloves, crushed
2.5ml/½ tsp allspice berries
2 bay leaves
2.5ml/½ tsp ground cumin
lime wedges, to serve

Variation
Ancho chillies are dried poblanos. They have a wonderful, slightly fruity aroma. If you prefer a smoky flavour, substitute mulato chillies.

1 Put the pork cubes in a large pan with water to cover. Bring to the boil, then simmer for 40 minutes. Meanwhile, heat the stock in a separate pan. Put the masa harina into a large bowl and add the hot stock, a little at a time, to make a stiff dough.

2 Put the lard in another bowl and beat with an electric whisk until light and fluffy, and a small amount dropped into a cup of water floats. Continue to beat the lard, gradually adding the masa dough, until the mixture is light and spreadable. Beat in the salt. Cover closely with clear film (plastic wrap) to stop the mixture from drying out.

3 Soak the corn husks in a bowl of cold water for 10 minutes. Drain, wipe off the white residue from the leaves, then soak in boiling water for 30 minutes. Soak the seeded chillies in a separate bowl of hot water for the same time. Drain the pork, reserving 105ml/7 tbsp of the cooking liquid, and chop the meat finely.

4 Heat the oil in a large pan and fry the onion and garlic for 2–3 minutes. Drain the chillies, chop them finely and add them to the pan.

5 Put the allspice berries and bay leaves in a mortar, grind them with a pestle, then work in the ground cumin. Add this to the onion mixture and stir well. Cook for 2–3 minutes more. Add the chopped pork and reserved cooking liquid and continue cooking until all the liquid has been absorbed. Cool slightly.

6 Drain the corn husks and pat them dry. Place one on a board. Spoon about one-twelfth of the masa mixture on to the centre of the husk wrapper and spread it almost to the sides. Place a spoonful of the meat mixture on top of the masa.

7 Fold the two long sides of the husk over the filling, then bring up each of the two shorter sides in turn, to make a neat parcel. Tie with long strips of corn husk or string.

8 Steam the tamales over simmering water for 1 hour, topping up the water as needed. To test if the tamales are ready, unwrap one. The filling should peel away from the husk cleanly. Pile the tamales on a plate, leave to stand for 10 minutes, then serve with lime wedges.

Lotus-wrapped sticky rice and chicken parcels

Their large size makes lotus leaves excellent wrappers. In Asia, where they grow, they are used for both savoury and sweet mixtures. Here, they hold a tasty marinated chicken filling.

Serves four

- 450g/1lb/2 cups glutinous rice
- 20ml/4 tsp sunflower oil
- 15ml/1 tbsp dark soy sauce
- 1.5ml/¼ tsp five-spice powder
- 15ml/1 tbsp dry sherry
- 4 skinless and boneless chicken thighs, each cut into 4 pieces
- 8 dried Chinese mushrooms, soaked in hot water until soft
- 25g/1oz dried shrimps, soaked in hot water until soft
- 50g/2oz/½ cup drained canned bamboo shoots, sliced
- 300ml/½ pint/1¼ cups chicken stock
- 10ml/2 tsp cornflour (cornstarch)
- 15ml/1 tbsp cold water
- 4 lotus leaves, soaked in warm water until soft
- salt and ground white pepper

1 Rinse the glutinous rice under running water until the water runs clear, then leave to soak in water for 2 hours. Drain, tip into a bowl and stir in 5ml/1 tsp of the oil and 2.5ml/½ tsp salt.

2 Line a large steamer with clean muslin (cheesecloth), then spoon the rice into it. Cover and steam over boiling water for about 45 minutes, stirring the rice occasionally and topping up the water if necessary.

3 Make a marinade by mixing the soy sauce, five-spice powder and sherry in a bowl. Put the chicken pieces in a shallow dish, pour over the marinade and turn to coat the chicken in the mixture. Cover and leave to marinate for 20 minutes.

4 Drain the Chinese mushrooms, cut out and discard the stems, then finely chop the caps. Drain the dried shrimps. Heat the remaining oil in a wok and gently stir-fry the chicken for 2 minutes. Add the mushrooms, shrimps, bamboo shoots and stock. Simmer for 10 minutes.

5 Mix the cornflour to a paste with the cold water. Add the mixture to the wok and cook, stirring, until the sauce has thickened. Add salt and white pepper to taste. Lift the cooked rice out of the steamer and let it cool slightly.

6 With slightly dampened hands, divide the rice into four equal portions. Put half of one portion in the centre of a lotus leaf. Spread it into a round and place one-quarter of the chicken mixture on top. Cover with the remaining portion of rice. Fold the leaf around the filling to make a neat rectangular parcel. Make three more parcels in the same way.

7 Prepare a steamer. Put the parcels, seam side down, in the steamer. Cover and steam over medium heat for about 30 minutes, then transfer the parcels to individual plates and serve. Guests open their own parcels at the table.

Steamed sole lettuce wraps

Lettuce makes an attractive wrap, and has a delicate texture and subtle flavour that makes it ideally suited to light fish mixtures such as this one.

Serves four

2 large sole or flounder fillets, skinned
15ml/1 tbsp sesame seeds
15ml/1 tbsp sunflower oil
10ml/2 tsp sesame oil
2.5cm/1in piece of fresh root ginger, peeled and grated
3 garlic cloves, finely chopped
15ml/1 tbsp soy sauce or fish sauce, plus extra, to serve
juice of 1 lemon
1 spring onion (scallion), thinly sliced
8 large soft lettuce leaves
12 large fresh mussels, scrubbed and bearded
salt and ground black pepper
4 lengths of spring onion (scallion) green, blanched and tied in small bows, to garnish (optional)

Variation
Dover sole is ideal for this dish, but trout, plaice and brill could also be used.

1 Cut the sole or flounder fillets in half lengthways. Season well and set aside. Prepare a steamer. Heat a heavy frying pan. When it is hot, sprinkle the sesame seeds evenly over the surface and toast them lightly. Do not let them burn. Tip into a bowl and set aside.

2 Heat both oils in the frying pan over a medium heat. Add the ginger and garlic and cook until lightly coloured, then stir in the soy sauce or fish sauce with the lemon juice and spring onion. Remove from the heat, add the toasted sesame seeds and stir well.

3 Lay a piece of fish, skin side up, on a board or square of baking parchment. Spread evenly with the ginger mixture, then roll up, starting at the tail end. Repeat with the remaining fish and filling.

4 Carefully plunge the lettuce leaves into the boiling water in the pan below the steamer. Immediately lift them out, using tongs or a slotted spoon. Lay them flat on kitchen paper and gently pat them dry. Wrap each fish roll in two lettuce leaves, making sure that the filling is well covered to keep it in place.

5 Arrange the fish parcels in the steamer basket, cover and steam over simmering water for 8 minutes. Add the mussels and steam for 2–4 minutes, until they have opened. Discard any that remain closed.

6 Carefully cut each parcel in half and arrange two halves on each serving plate, placing them flat so that the filling can be seen clearly. Drizzle a little of the soy sauce or fish sauce around and place three mussels on each plate. Garnish with bows of spring onion green, if you like.

Cook's tip
To make the spring onion (scallion) bows for the garnish, cut thin strips of spring onion green. Soften them if necessary by blanching them briefly in boiling water. Drain and tie in bows.

Hand-rolled sushi

Quite the easiest way to serve sushi, this involves setting out all the filling ingredients with accompaniments and nori wraps. It's a great ice-breaker for guests at a dinner party.

Serves four to six

225g/8oz extremely fresh tuna steak
130g/4½oz smoked salmon
17cm/6½in salad cucumber
8 raw king prawns (jumbo shrimp) or large tiger prawns, peeled and heads removed
1 avocado
7.5ml/1½ tsp lemon juice
20 fresh chives, chopped into 6cm/2½in lengths
1 packet mustard and cress, leaves cut from roots, or land cress
6–8 shiso leaves, halved lengthways

For the vinegared rice

400g/14oz/2 cups Japanese short grain rice
40ml/8 tsp sugar
7.5ml/1½ tsp salt
45ml/3 tbsp rice vinegar

To serve

12 nori sheets, each cut in four
45ml/3 tbsp wasabi paste
soy sauce
gari (pickled ginger)

1 Make the vinegared rice. Rinse the rice in a sieve under plenty of cold running water until the water runs clear. Allow to drain for 1 hour, then put it in a pan. Pour in 250ml/8fl oz/1 cup water, cover and bring to the boil. Lower the heat and simmer for 12 minutes without lifting the lid. Remove from the heat and leave for 10 minutes.

2 Spoon the rice into a large bowl. Dissolve the sugar and salt in the vinegar, then fold the mixture into the hot rice, using a wet fish slice (metal spatula). Cover and leave to cool.

3 Slice the tuna, with the grain, into 5mm/¼in slices, then into 1 x 6cm/½ x 2½in strips. Cut the salmon and cucumber into strips the same size as the tuna.

4 Insert bamboo skewers along the length of the prawns to keep them straight, then boil in lightly salted water for 2 minutes. Drain and leave to cool. Remove the skewers and, using a small, sharp knife, cut in half lengthways. Remove the vein from each prawn.

5 Halve, stone (pit) and peel the avocado. Sprinkle with half the lemon juice and cut into 1cm/½in long strips. Sprinkle on the remaining lemon juice. Arrange the fish, shellfish, avocado, chives, cress and shiso leaves on a plate.

6 Pile up the nori sheets on a platter and spoon the wasabi paste, soy sauce and gari into separate bowls. Half-fill a glass with water and place a rice paddle or dessertspoon for each guest inside. Arrange everything on the table.

7 Invite guests to roll their own sushi, following your example. Place a sheet of nori on your palm, then scoop out 45ml/3 tbsp of vinegared rice and spread it on the nori. Dot a small amount of wasabi in the middle of the rice, then put a few strips of different fillings on top. Roll the nori around the filling to make a cone and dip the end in the soy sauce. It is traditional to cleanse the mouth between rolls by eating a little of the gari.

Coffee crêpes with peaches and cream

To wrap up a sophisticated meal, try these sumptuous crêpes with juicy peaches and clouds of amaretto cream. The liqueur perfectly complements the coffee flavour.

Serves six

75g/3oz/¾ cup plain (all-purpose) flour
25g/1oz/¼ cup buckwheat flour
1.5ml/¼ tsp salt
1 egg, beaten
200ml/7fl oz/scant 1 cup milk
15g/½oz/1 tbsp butter, melted
100ml/3½fl oz/scant ½ cup strong brewed coffee
sunflower oil, for frying
30ml/2 tbsp icing (confectioners') sugar, for dusting, optional

For the filling

6 ripe peaches
300ml/½ pint/1¼ cups double (heavy) cream
15ml/1 tbsp amaretto liqueur
225g/8oz/1 cup mascarpone
75ml/5 tbsp caster (superfine) sugar

1 Sift the flours and salt into a mixing bowl. Make a well in the middle and add the egg, half the milk and the melted butter. Gently beat the liquids, gradually incorporating the surrounding flour, until smooth, then beat in the remaining milk and the coffee to make a batter.

2 Heat a drizzle of oil in a 15–20cm/ 6–8in crêpe pan. Pour in just enough batter to cover the base thinly. Cook for 2–3 minutes, until golden, then flip the crêpe over and cook the other side.

3 Slide the crêpe out of the pan on to a plate. Continue making crêpes until all the mixture has been used, stacking the cooked crêpes and interleaving them with baking parchment.

4 To make the filling, halve the peaches and remove the stones (pits). Cut into slices. Whip the cream and amaretto liqueur until soft peaks form. Beat the mascarpone with the sugar until smooth. Beat 30ml/2 tbsp of the cream into the mascarpone, then fold in the remainder.

5 Spoon a little of the amaretto cream on to one half of each crêpe and top with peach slices. Gently fold the crêpe over and dust generously with icing sugar, if you wish. Serve immediately.

Cook's tip
Look out for packs of pancakes in the supermarket. Both plain pancakes and large French crêpes are available. Reheat them before filling.

Cranberry sorbet in lace pancakes

This stunning dessert contrasts colour and texture with its combination of vibrant red sorbet in wispy pancakes. Dust with icing sugar for an elegant finishing touch.

Serves six

500g/1¼lb/5 cups cranberries
225g/8oz/generous 1 cup sugar
300ml/½ pint/1¼ cups orange juice
60ml/4 tbsp Cointreau or other orange-flavoured liqueur
icing (confectioners') sugar for dusting
extra cranberries and lightly whipped cream (optional), to serve

For the pancakes

50g/2oz/½ cup plain (all-purpose) flour
2.5ml/½ tsp ground ginger
1 egg
15ml/1 tbsp caster (superfine) sugar
120ml/4fl oz/½ cup milk
a little oil, for frying

Variation

When you are in a hurry, use bought sorbet and pancakes. If you want to recreate the lacy effect, use a vegetable cutter to cut out shapes from the pancakes.

1 Put the cranberries, sugar and orange juice in a pan and heat gently until the sugar has dissolved. Cover and cook gently for 5–8 minutes more, until the cranberries are very tender. Leave to cool.

2 Tip the mixture into a food processor and process until very smooth. Press the purée through a sieve placed over a bowl to extract as much juice as possible. Stir the liqueur into the juice, then chill until it is very cold.

3 Pour the mixture into a shallow freezerproof container and freeze for 3–4 hours, beating twice to break up the ice crystals. Alternatively, make the sorbet in an ice-cream maker, then scrape into a suitable container. Freeze the sorbet overnight.

4 Make the pancakes. Sift the flour and ginger into a bowl. Add the egg, sugar and a little of the milk. Gradually whisk in the remaining milk to make a smooth batter. Heat a little oil in a small frying pan or crêpe pan. Pour off the excess oil and remove the pan from the heat.

5 Using a dessertspoon, drizzle a little of the batter over the base of the hot pan, using a scribbling action to create a pancake that looks like a lacy doily and measures about 14cm/5½in across. Make sure that all the lacy edges are connected around the edge of the pancake. Return the pan to the heat and cook the pancake until golden on the underside.

6 Carefully turn the lace pancake over and cook for 1 minute more. Slide on to a plate and leave to cool. Make five more pancakes in the same way, lightly oiling the pan each time. To serve, lay a pancake on a dessert plate and arrange several small scoops of sorbet on one side. Fold the pancake over and dust with the icing sugar. Sprinkle with extra cranberries and serve with whipped cream, if you wish.

Index

a
apple wraps with butterscotch sauce 44
Asian pancakes 8, 11
    Peking duck with mandarin pancakes 50
aubergine, tomato and mozzarella wraps 26

b
beef enchiladas 40
bread wraps 9
    panettone rolls with mascarpone and crushed berries 28
    roasted vegetable lavash wrap 32
bulgur wheat: lamb kebab wraps 48
burritos 10
    red snapper burritos 42
butterscotch sauce, apple wraps with 44

c
California wrap 16
chapatis 8, 11
cheese: aubergine, tomato and mozzarella wraps 26
    panettone rolls with mascarpone and crushed berries 28
    tortilla cones with smoked salmon and soft cheese 18
chicken: chicken and tomatillo chimichangas 38
    lotus-wrapped sticky rice and chicken parcels 54
chimichangas 10
    chicken and tomatillo chimichangas 38
coffee crêpes with peaches and cream 60
coriander omelette wraps 36
corn husks 9, 11
    tamales filled with spiced pork 52
courgettes, Moroccan spiced 48
crab: California wrap 16
cranberry sorbet in lace pancakes 62
crêpes 9, 11
    coffee crêpes with peaches and cream 60

d
dipping sauces, 13
duck: Peking duck with mandarin pancakes 50

e
enchiladas 10
    beef enchiladas 40

f
fajitas 10
flautas 10

l
lamb kebab wraps 48
leaves 9
lettuce leaves 9
    steamed sole lettuce wraps 56
lotus leaves 9
    lotus-wrapped sticky rice and chicken parcels 54

n
nori 9
    hand-rolled sushi 58

o
omelette wraps, coriander 36

p
pancakes 9, 11
    cranberry sorbet in lace pancakes 62
    Vietnamese rice paper rolls 22
    see also Asian pancakes
panettone rolls with mascarpone and crushed berries 28
peaches, coffee crêpes with 60
Peking duck with mandarin pancakes 50
pork: crispy Shanghai spring rolls 20
    tamales filled with spiced pork 52
prawns: crispy Shanghai spring rolls 20

q
quesadillas 10

r
red mullet dolmades 24
red snapper burritos 42
rice: hand-rolled sushi 58
    lotus-wrapped sticky rice and chicken parcels 54

s
sauces, dipping 13
smoked salmon, tortilla cones with soft cheese 18
sole: steamed sole lettuce wraps 56
spinach leaves 9
spring rolls, crispy Shanghai 20
sushi, hand-rolled 58

t
tamales filled with spiced pork 52
tomato tortillas with pancetta and caramelized red onions 34
tortillas 8, 10
    apple wraps with butterscotch sauce 44
    beef enchiladas 40
    California wrap 16
    chicken and tomatillo chimichangas 38
    lamb kebab wraps 48
    red snapper burritos 42
    tomato tortillas with pancetta and caramelized red onions 34
    tortilla cones with smoked salmon and soft cheese 18

v
vegetables: coriander omelette wraps 36
    roasted vegetable lavash wrap 32
Vietnamese rice paper rolls 22
vine leaves 9
    red mullet dolmades 24